From Okra
to Greens /

A Different
Kinda Love Story

A Play with Music & Dance

by Ntozake Shange

A SAMUEL FRENCH ACTING EDITION

SAMUEL FRENCH

FOUNDED 1830

New York Hollywood London Toronto

SAMUELFRENCH.COM

FROM OKRA TO GREENS was originally performed (under the title MOUTHS) at The Kitchen, New York City, in April, 1981, with the following personnel: Ntozake Shange, Richard Lawson, Halifu Osimare, Ed Monk, and Elvia Marta. Directed by Thulani Davis, Choreography by Diane McIntyre, Set Design (drawings) by Ntozake Shange, Costumes by Marion ViCaires. Produced by John Woo in association with the Basement Workshop. It was subsequently performed as part of THREE FOR A FULL MOON at the Mark Taper Theater Lab.

DEDICATION

for savannah thulani-éloisa, my daughter & our grandmothers/
Eloise Owens Williams & Martha Binion
   Viola Benzena Murray Owens & Ida B. Williams our godmothers
   Thulani Davis, Jessica Hagedorn,
Nanette Bearden & Gail Merrifield
      Margaret Sullivan & Katie Moore
My sisters/ her aunts
      Wanda & Bisa
My brother/ her uncle
      Paul
My father/ her grandfather, 'Boppy'
      Paul Towbin Williams, M.D.

****

Ahora que tu has huelto
de recío de humo
lágrima i lágrima

Y que es tu vas apenas
láud, metal lejano
lágrima y lágrima

De tu cintura hacen
las siempremas
lágrima y lágrima

Una paloma oscure
me persigue y te nambia

Lágrima. Lágrimas.

Rafaela Chacon Nardi

(*Martinez Inoforza
Editorial Letras Cubanas
Ciudad de La Habana, Cuba, 1982*)

4

CAST

OKRA — Afro-American woman
GREENS — Afro-American man
FIVE DANCERS — The people of their worlds

From Okra to Greens/
A Different Kinda Love Story

The stage is bare, except for a highly textured and vibrant backdrop that echoes of Africa and the Aztec Empire. There is nothing suggesting modern times or urban civilization. From the sides and through the back, ALL SEVEN (7) CHARAC-TERS appear at the sound of a gong, reminescent of Sikh meditations. In slow motion they assemble in the middle of the stage. The CHARACTERS are dressed in the garb of slaves in the New World (Brazil, Martinique, Haiti, Mexico, North America). They begin a dance that is traditionally African. The movements may be drawn from the Ashanti, Yoruba, or Ewe tribes. This is a dance of celebration. The dance approaches Nirvanic heights at which top point, all dancers, except OKRA and GREENS, dance off the stage.
A violent saxophone solo of short duration anticipates GREEN's opening speech. He becomes very street-wise and English-speaking Afro-American cynical, as OKRA acts out the physical and emotional distortions of "the crooked woman."

GREENS.
the woman dont stand up
straight
aint never stood up
straight/ always bent
some which a way
crooked   turned abt

7

slanted sorta toward
a shadow of herself
seems like she
tryin to get all in the
ground/ wit the death
of her
somethin always on her
shoulders/ pushin
her outta herself
cuttin at her limbs
a wonder she cd
stand at all/ seein
how she waz all curled over herself
a greetin sent her chin
neath her arm/ a
smile chased her neck
tween her legs/
waznt just she cdnt stand up straight/
she cdnt
hardly keep somebody
else's body outta hers
& since everyone cd
see/ immediately/ this
child always bends over
always twists
round herself to
keep from standin up
folks wd just go play
wit her/ get they kicks
watchin the crooked lady
do her thing/ & her bones
gotta crackin
shatterin/ mutilatin
themselves til she

waz lookin so weird
to herself she
locked herself up in
a closet/ where she
met a man/ she musta made up/
cuz he didnt know what a stood
up straight man felt like/
in the dark
we curled round/
nobody cd tell anymore/ what to
get outta the way of/ & we
never once spoke/
of our condition.

(*OKRA moves sensually from her embrace with
GREENS to begin: "You are sucha gool."
Throughout this piece vernacular black dance steps
may be introduced.*)

OKRA.
you are sucha fool/ i haveta love you
GREENS.
you decide to give me a poem/ intent on it/
actually
OKRA.
you pull/ kiss me from 125th to 72nd street/ on
the east side/ no less
GREENS.
you are sucha fool/ you gonna give me/ the poet/
the poem
OKRA.
insistin on proletarian images/ we buy okra/
3 lbs for $1/ & a pair of 98 cent shoes

GREENS.
we kiss
OKRA.
we wrestle
GREENS.
you make sure at east 110th street/ we have
   cognac   OKRA.
no beer all day
   GREENS.
you are sucha fool/ you fall over my day like
a wash of azure
   OKRA.
you take my tongue outta my mouth/
make me say foolish things
   GREENS.
you take my tongue outta my mouth/ lay it on yr
   skin
like the dew between yr legs
   OKRA.
on this the first day of silver balloons
& lil girl's braids undone
   GREENS.
friendly savage skulls on bikes/ wish me good-day
you speak spanish like a german & ask puerto rican
marketmen on lexington if they are foreigners
   OKRA.
oh you are sucha fool/ i cant help but love you
   GREENS.
maybe it was something in the air
   OKRA.
our memories
   GREENS.
our first walk

OKRA.
our first . . .
      GREENS.
yes/ alla that
      OKRA.
where you poured wine down my throat in rooms
poets i dreamed abt seduced sound & made history/
you make me feel like a cheetah
      GREENS.
a gazelle/ something fast & beautiful
      OKRA.
you make me remember my animal sounds/
so while i am an antelope
      GREENS.
ocelot & serpent speaking in tongues
      OKRA.
my body loosens for/ you
      GREENS.
you decide to give me the poem
      OKRA.
you wet yr finger/ lay it to my lips
that i might write some more abt you/
how you come   into me
      GREENS.
the way the blues jumps outta b.b. king/ how
david murray assaults a moon & takes her home/
like dyanne harvey invades the wind
      OKRA.
oh you/ you are sucha fool/
you want me to write some more abt you
      GREENS.
how i come into you like a rollercoaster in a
dip that swings

leave you shattered/ glistening/ rich/ screeching
& fully clothed
    OKRA.
you set me up to fall into yr dreams
    GREENS.
like the sub-saharan animal i am/ in all this heat
wanting to be still
    OKRA.
to be still with you
    GREENS.
in the shadows
    OKRA.
all those buildings
    GREENS.
all those people/ celebrating/ sunlight & love/
    you
    OKRA.
you are sucha fool/ you spend all day piling up
    images
locations/ morsels of daydreams/ to give me a poem
    GREENS.
just smile/ i'll get it
(*He exits.*)

*OKRA shares as if a secret the following. She moves
across the stage continually making sure that no one
(especially GREENS) can hear her, sharing with the
audience.*

    OKRA.
i haveta turn my television down sometimes cuz
i cant stand to have white people /shout at me/
sometimes i turn it off
cuz i cant look at em in my bedroom either/

bein so white/
that's why i like/greens/
they cdnt even smell you/ wdnt know what you taste
    like
without sneakin / got no
idea you shd be tingled wit hot sauce & showered wit
    vinegar
yr pot liquor spread on hot rolls

i gotta turn the TV off cuz the white people
keep playing games/ & folowin presidents on vacation
    at the war
there's too much of a odor problem on the TV too/
    which
brings me back to greens

i remember my grandma at the market pickin turnips
collards kale & mustards/ to mix-em up/ drop a ½
    of strick a lean
in there wit some ham hock & oh my whatta life/
i lived in her kitchen/ wit greens i cd recollect
yes the very root of myself
        the dirt & lil bugs i looked for in the fresh
            collards/
        turnin each leaf way so slow/ under the
            spicket/ watchin
        lil mounds of dirt fall down the drain
i done a good job
grandma tol me/ got them greens just ready for the
    pot
& you know/ wdnt no white man on the TV/
talkin loud n formal make no sense o the miracle
a good pot a greens on a friday nite cd make to me
that's only reason i turn em off the TV

cant stand they gossipin abt the news/ sides they
  dont
never like the criminals & enemies i like anyway
that's why i like GREENS/ i know how to cook em
& i sure can dream gd/ soppin up the pot liquor
& them peppers/

*(On OKRA's last line a tumultous somba rhythm is
heard. All the DANCERS appear. A traditional
Brazilian somba 'contest' is held between all
players. GREENS wins. He begins "Ita parica" as
he takes OKRA as the 'roze' of the event. The other
DANCERS saunter off slowly, hot with the elan of
carnival. GREENS heads OKRA about front,
showing her the Rio landscape as he understands it.
All the locations are in the direction of the audience. As the dual ends the other DANCERS enter
with a copoeira ritual that becomes ominous in its
violence. At this point, OKRA addresses GREENS.)*

OKRA.
     /at Asbury Park in october
all the bldgs fell thru
the earth got lil
our smiles swallowed the sky
GREENS.
itaparica is where doña flor
took her two husbands/ itaparica is where
giogo dos santos is nine years fulla mosquito bites
& will die soon
itaparica is not near corcuvado
     cristo redentor
nor the copacabana
where the children eat off the plates of tourists/

anything/ no
itaparica is not close to rocinha
behind the sheraton/ covered with tin, stolen
bricks & women's stooped shoulders
i know rocinha's the only favela
with a legal city sign:

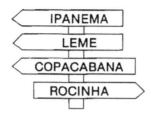

   OKRA.
a blue space opened tween
steel/ i lay on you
   GREENS.
itaparica is an island
a half-day's sail from salvador
one half-hour from itapuã
where the old man fries fish & counts money
         in his favor
his children row boats like in mindanao
like in mindanao/ they have forgotten
nothing
itapuã with a church on the highest hill
   OKRA.
synecdoche / out smiles swallowed the sky
   GREENS.
in land houses in curaçao
the safest place for slave owners

on crests of waves of slaves
who cd not move without being seen
   OKRA.
our lady of lourdes in jurujuba
collects crutches & back braces
itapuã collects tourists
throws them back to the sea
under the gaze of the master of christ's house/
tween itaparica & itapuã
   GREENS.
i found a calm
   OKRA.
a rinsing off of history too grimy
   GREENS.
a washing away of memories not fit for sleep
   OKRA.
a burnin salted cleansing
   GREENS.
i sailed/ i sailed on a schooner
smelling of fish/ whiskey & sweat
   OKRA.
i sailed to a samba
slept with the sea in a fit of petulance
consorted with winds rough as avenue 'c'
   GREENS.
you climbed from those stars
   OKRA.
tween itaparica & itapuã
   GREENS.
you sat up in the sky/ began to strut around
yr legs swept thru the night/ you took the
half-moon in yr hands/ twirled her
a pinwheel/ for me

OKRA.
you settled on a armful of stars
took me to a harbor
   GREENS.
some visions slip outta trees
   OKRA.
others stalk the lakes inland
   GREENS.
others leap from the glory of the sun
   OKRA.
you stood up in the night/ yr palms pushing stars
to fall in delerium/ letting me know
all i see is true
   GREENS.
we are as impregnable as night/ as dangerous
   OKRA.
i sailed to a samba
   GREENS.
tween itaparica & itapuã
   OKRA.
you walked across the sky
to give me a safe harbor
   GREENS.
i slept with the sea in a fit of petulance
   OKRA.
you climbed from the stars
in yr new straw hat
   GREENS.
clouds we cd walk on
   OKRA.
shadows race behind
   GREENS.
pickin up what's left

OKRA.
the earth got little
GREENS.
our smiles swallowed the sky

(*The DANCERS exit to all corners in intensely stylized
movement. OKRA and GREENS are alone as if in a
bedroom. Yet when GREENS begins "he was a
pretty little man" one DANCER enters dressed in
the manner of "Vanity" or "Apollonia." She acts
out all the narrative as OKRA exits, on "this was an
honor."*)

OKRA.
some/ men
dont know anything abt that.
the manliness inherent at birth
is lost as they grow or shrink
to size
some/ men
dont know that a well dressed man
is a good female impersonator
that machines replace them & do a better job
some/ men
have no language that doesnt hurt
a language that doesnt reduce what's whole
to some part of nothing
sometimes/ some men think
it's funny/ really funny
women have anything to do with them
GREENS.
he was a pretty man who liked pretty things.
surrounded with beat-up luxuries/ old mantillas
from women's heads lay cross his mahogany tables/

bronze nymphs, bulbs in their mouths, lit up
his quarters/ onyx vases steadied scarlet tulips
    before
french windows he opened when he had expresso
in early morning
he kept a dressing gown/ mauve dotted with black
    velvet.
he waxed his floors til they shone & covered them
    with
near eastern rugs/ the kind little girls spend whole
lives tying.
he walked about grandly.
though he was a little man/ he liked to think
    himself
          large.
he had so many pretty things.
he never bent his knees/ that added some inches
& kept him from looking anyone in the eye
          there'd be nothing new in his visions.
old pretty things/ used abused beauties
like the women who decorated his bed from time to
    time.
he sat them on old sheets & displayed the dusty
manuscripts he collected/ the vintage photographs
he stored/ the women passt   whose legs he'd pulled
over his hips like a holster.
this was an honor
to lay naked with a pretty man among his pretty
    things/
the violated thrown-out pieces of lives he recovered
from rummages   scavaging & gutters.
the beauty of it all
was it cost him so little. imagine him
so small a man getting away with all that.

nothing new. not a new   thing.
what's to value in something unblemished?
porcelain must be cracked/ to covet. rugs frayed/
to desire. there must be scratches on the surfaces/
to enjoy what's beautiful.
he was really very tiny in the big brass bed.
the beauty of the woman overpowered him. she didn't
even seem to be afraid in the presence of all his
pretty things.
he thought of the most beautiful thing he cd say.
what words wd match his pretty little face.
what phrase to approach the sunlight mad with joy
on the limbs of this woman next to him.
what he could do so perfectly.
he was a little man
& straightening his legs in the bed added nothing to
his stature. he sat up & crushed the frailty of
the morning
     "suck my dick & make some coffee"
he squealed.
she ran out
with no more than her coat/ with her shoes in her
    hands
keys in her mouth. she thought she must have lost
her mind.
but
he was a small man
& cd handle only damaged goods. he sat in his big
    bed
with his little legs bent/ quite content.
now/ there was something someone else cd collect/
an abused/ used luxury/ a woman
with a memory of daybreak in a near perfect place/
sunlight warm against her face & a man squeaking
suck my dick & make some coffee

(*DANCER exits.*)
she always woke before her lovers/ after that.
she never slept near windows/ & the aroma of coffee
left her pale.
& he was a little man/ a pretty man
surrounded with beat-up luxuries/ creating blemishes
scratches   fraying edges/ illusions
of filling the bed he slept in
(*GREENS exits.*)
   OKRA.
it was best to call in the middle of the night.
women living alone are startled by noises at late
   hours.
it is best to ring twice & hang up.
then ring back/ say nothing.
women living alone are familiar with perversions.
he decided to ring twice & hang up three times.
he felt once she answered/ heard a man breathing/
she'd hang up quickly.
then
he cd call back & she'd be so glad
finally a man she knew
a man she cd trust in the middle of the night.

(*OKRA starts to exit, but GREENS pulls her back in.*)

   GREENS.
he said/   she had too much for her own good.
too much what/   she asked
everything/   he said
but what/   she asked
money/   he shouted/   too much money
yeah/ too much energy/ just too much/ you/
dont need all that.   you should give it to me
i'm a man/   he said

she said nothing
he turned around.
his eyes sparkled when he told her what she really
needed to do was have a baby/   she needed
something to tie her down.
· OKRA. (*hostiley, stalking GREENS*)
there was nothing he could see in a woman that was
of any use at all. she was forever silly.
look at that mess you put on yr face/ why dont you
use kohl like algerian women/ why dont you cover
your face
everytime she'd try to do what pleased him/
he'd find a more indelicate failure.
what's wrong with your hair?   dont you oil your
    legs?
why do you let your pussy hair grow so long/ cut it
    off!
get your teeth fixed/ sit over there &
take your pants off.
he liked pornographic still-lifes.
when he cant afford the quarter machine/ he invites
    women
to keep him company/ then he makes them ugly.
    GREENS. (*stalking OKRA*)
he kept the place empty. so no one wd ever imagine
that a woman lived there/ which is what he wanted
for no one to know.
if she lived empty & angular as he did, she'd become
less a woman & part of the design/ where anything he
wanted to happen/ happened.
    OKRA.
the baby gets up every hour & a half. she's a spunky
little baby who cries & smiles a lot. she needs to
    nurse

& her mama's right there. without sleep or no/ the
  milk flows.
          he doesnt like that.   he said.
there's no one taking care of me.   he thought
her stitches shd heal faster. she shdnt take so
many sitz baths.   she takes too long to walk from
  here to
there/ she doesnt actually haveta walk funny like
  that
it dont hurt her/ it wont hurt/ he said/ it wdnt
  hurt.
dont you remember before that damned baby? it was
  me.
it was me & you. there's always milk for the baby
none for me/ never too tired for the baby/ never too
tired for the baby/ he didnt understand
why she sat on the stairway crying all night with
  the
spunky little baby
he hadnt done nothing but hold her arms back/ & bite
on her titties/ how did he know his teeth wd hurt
how cd he know/ shit/ she always has time for the
  baby
what was he sposed to do/ the milk flows whether
  she tired
or not/ when was he gonna get some/ he said it wont
  hurt/
it wont hurt/ dont you remember . . .
(*She leaves in terror and pain.*)
     GREENS. (*arrogant and nasty*)
he waited
          til she got out of her car
& pulled his dick out   exactly 6 ft
from her doorway.

the car was locked
the front door was locked
there was a man with his dick out
freezin winds
her hands trembling/ her mouth falling over her
   scalp
his laughter came all over her coat

(*He is laughing. OKRA returns, timidly.*)

OKRA. (*delicately*)
he looked at the flowers on her window sill/
roses, lilacs, lilies & mums.   the flowers
on her curtains/ blazing tropical petals
& stamen
   GREENS. (*Entranced by the beauty of her images;
they are lovers again.*)
her desk festooned with strange cacti & terrarium.
she had covered her ceilings in arcs of ivy/
made herself a garden full of soft round shapes/
fragrance & manners.
   OKRA.
he felt her thighs/ strong & wet.
her body arching like ferns reaching/ she was
   smiling
& feverish with desire
   GREENS.
      strange sounds fell from her mouth
gurgling innocent hot sounds/ crept along his back
her fingers
   OKRA.
sought out the hairs long his neck/
   GREENS.
the evening fog laced kisses round their bodies/

OKRA.
she thought she heard piano solos/ she thought she
    heard
trumpets gone marvelously wild in nature's
    murmurings
GREENS.
            she felt him coming
OKRA.
& let go all her powers
GREENS.
when without warning
he shot all his semen up her ass
    OKRA.
she kept screaming
WHAT ARE YOU DOING WHAT ARE YOU DOING
    to me
    GREENS.'
he relaxed/ sighing
            "i had to put it somewhere. it was
too good to be some pussy."
    OKRA.
some men would rather see us dead than imagine
what we think of them/
if we measure our silence by our pain
how could all the words
any word
ever catch up
what is it we cd call equal

(*All DANCERS re-enter to do an improvised dance of
    violence and revenge.*)

    GREENS. (*hesitatingly approaching OKRA:*)
in the middle of the nite

is a blue thing
a blue thing in the nite
which covers me
makes music
like leaves that havent shown/
themselves &
when i dont know where i am
when i dont know when i'll see you
what time it is
i lay
in the middle of the nite
covered up with   this   blue-ness
this memory of you

some poets' eyes see hazel

mine see/ blue
sometimes it moves/ actually rocks
so even paris is not quiet
for me/ i linger by the seine
une femme brune
bein blue like the velvet hips
of river biguine for me
sway in the thickness
air on my arms
holdin me in from the nite i cd
enter with you
in the blueness
the forever weight of yr arms
mine filled with sky

here i am carryin yr lips
yr tune now/ how you sing me
sometimes i even see clouds run

long like sea/ throw me like waves
throw me like wind/ make our breath
like the earth turnin/
never stoppin never hummin
but so loud

(*The DANCERS reappear in a deep blue light doing a
ritualistic Arabic movement with shoulders and
head swings. They surround OKRA and GREENS
and leave them.*)

OKRA.
what language is it in
when my bed is /   too big   cuz yr not in it
how cd i say
my snyapses remember where yr lips
linger/ unaccompanied bach/ sometimes you
are angolan freedom songs/ we take all
confusions & raggae it/ tosh marley & wailer/
we stroll in our own convers all-stars/ in
london & são paulo/ but what language is it
big enough/to say yr name
how many colors is the sound of you put to
    skies/ dusk/ in amber & midnite reds/
if i say yr name wd the words roll like pomegranates
from everyone's mouth/ what language fits our needs
we are so far gone / we dont know sanskrit
i dont want a saxophone/i like greens
say how to reach you so i am clear/
you'd know pearl harbor day/ bastille day/ the
day they invaded cambodia / is known to you/
all that death/ all the bleedin & screams/ are
    clear/
say how to reach you with love/ i am like air

now/ everywhere / speakin / whispers behind yr back
around the corner/ talkin abt you/ upstairs
in hushes/ yr name/ i stop you outside
deux maggots/ i say simply/
give me yr tongue/ darling
(*GREENS coyly exits.*)

(*Three MALE DANCERS slowly put themselves in a
triangle in the stance of the victorous liberators, of
Haiti: Dessalers, petion and L'Ouverture. OKRA
addresses the dancers who are posed as statues. She
moves in and about them. The statues change to
become the peasants and the crippled and then
again themselves when OKRA begins the long
French chant "ou sent-ils   maintenant ?" There is
a strong dance of liberation after OKRA's exit in
the middle of the 2nd refrain of the French verse
beginning on page 00. This dance is a major state-
ment in the piece: Militaristic & powerful.*)

OKRA.
the sailor/ le marin/ tells me
"there is no violence in haiti.
        jamaica has so many problems
the black people here are 'la majorite'."
the children are begging
        "lady give me something"
they make his heart sick
he sails yachts for italians hiding from the red
    brigade
he thinks you're cute & exotic/ even
i think of brazilians/ on emancipation
sailing back to dahomey/ he sails yachts
from capetown to rio/ charters for the french

americans have so lil class
the begging children make his heart sick
dessalines/ are the women sleeping at yr feet
bothersome/ does yr marble horse smell there fatigue
the mensis & milk at noon
the old man with one leg/ one hand/ one
elbow/ does he offend yr
sensibilities
on these great marble horses
will you come again/ some one of you
sweep thru the alleys & the stink/ come here
with yr visions
la liberté. l'égalité. la fraternité.
come visit among us that we might know
again/ some hope
port-au-prince is a rough town
le boulevard jean-jacques dessalines
a desecration/ les haitiennes paint
like niggahs in philadelphia love to dance/
all over the roads/ paradise jumps
from canvas/ to be sold to tourists/ to take abroad
petion/ l'ouverture/ dessalines
on horseback/ will you ride back
thru here/ invoke those same spirits
you called on at the citadel/ there are half-naked
women sleeping at yr feet/ children begging under yr
bridled stallions/ what 3 horses wd balk at/ one
    black man
carries on his back/ his sweat falls into the
    streams
of blood/ the yng men spit up
on the boulevard jean-jacques dessalines
papa doc made it possible
duvalier hadda lotta ju ju hoodoo grisgris

weapons
duvalier insisted/ the black people
cd go everywhere
aux téâtres   aux restaurants   aux musées/ to hell
his son lights up le palais national like christmas
in new york/ every night
the secret police come out in their trucks/ to scour
nos voisins/ our neighborhoods
can you stand it?
can you stand it, dessalines?
can you stand it, pétion/ l'ouverture?
can you stand these children
with the red eyes & dacron brazzieres for sale?
do you believe all the prostitutes/ in la fiesta
are from santo domingo/ les vaches espagnoles?
les vaches espagnoles?
now/ marius tresor is an international hero
he plays soccer & sleeps with a blonde
do you ride yr horses for him?
do you salute the deformed of port-au-prince
with yr plumed hats & swords?
what are you doing on those goddamned horses?
cant you see these old women hobbling abt
like mares abt to be shot/ leaning on fences
by the palais national?
jean-claude invokes the spirits & disgraces
le negre marron who awready ran away from
    slavery
in santo domingo/ to catch the tears
of these children/ who have so lil will
they dont even steal . . .
dessalines/ pétion/ l'ouverture
you must come back
start all over again

no one will move
(*Here dance begins. OKRA chants. She repeats as many times as choreographer desires.*)
personne ne bouge pas sans la puissance des dieux
vous les connaissez/ venez ici
tes enfants ne savent que la mort
tes femmes marchent avec la faim
tes hommes travaillent sans raison
tex vieux sont fatigués
what are you doing on those marble horses?
l'haiti a besoin
l'haiti a besoin/ de la liberté/ l'égalité/
    fraternité
l'haiti/ le premier pays au monde sans esclaves
l'haiti/ la nation de l'independance noire
what is going on/ here?
ou est dessalines/ maintenant?
ou est pétion/ l'ouverture?
ou sont-ils qui peuvent nous aider à la liberté
l'égalité/ la fraternité?
ou sont-ils maintenant/ l'haiti a besoin
(*The Haitians exit.*)

(*GREENS enters & joins dance. The other DANCERS
    exit.*)

GREENS.
i dreamed myself in a house of yr paintings
fore you even said diagonally yes
yrs/ mine   you/ me/   this cant be simple
this is non-fiction
most of the world is make-believe & predictable

(*OKRA enters from audience.*)

OKRA.
our latitudes & longitudes have other names
fiction/ non-fiction
you understand all this/ where did the question go?
he's lost/ in the office of protocol/ check with me
for verification/ my fiction file is in gd shape
i know a lotta novelists who stock up my drawers
    with
tales to be put away/ song writers who   are mute &
tone deaf/ leave their lyrics in the milkcan
    outside/
somewhere in l.a. private security guards stop
    motorists
& force em to pick up rumors/ non-fictionally
i'm harder to reach
    GREENS.
you cd try direct
when i'm vulnerable & survivin
i get each moment back/ i want to know
what we make
in the world/ survivin us/ makes us
(*They meet.*)
    OKRA.
non-fiction/ unless yr holdin back
then you are fiction & i am a plot
so my silence is a kind of gratitude
how often am i understood if i open my mouth
    GREENS.
we give each other empty paper bags & ticket stubs
we've been someplaces or are going
this is not camp
    OKRA.
this is a wide open hand/ unsettled unclaimed
in the hinterlands or ordinary / we cd homestead

we cd parcel it off to former levittowners
we cd put a hold on it/ we cd save it til the next
    time
we cd burrow our feet in soil & gather up sky wine
    & music
    GREENS.
you know whatta breeze is at twilight in autumn
    OKRA.
the horizon lays out in violet & sepia
    GREENS.
jets of orange wisk thru our hands
    OKRA.
that's why my neck gets so hot when you touch me
    GREENS.
the last heavy breaths of day belong to us
    OKRA.
non-fiction/

(*The DANCERS run rapidly and desparately across the
    stage immediately after OKRA says "non-fiction"
    (32). They are dressed as children. They are afraid.
    GREENS catches one of the girls and begins "cuz
    she's black and poor." He lets her go gently, yet
    vehemently continues the dialogue with OKRA.*)

    GREENS.
cuz she's black & poor
she's disappeared
her name is lost   games weren't played
nobody tucks her in / wipes traces of
cornbread & syrup from her lips
cuz she's black & poor / she's not.

just gone   disappeared one day

& her blood soaks what's awready red in atlanta
   OKRA.
no ropes this time   no tar & feathers
weren't no parades of sheets fires &
crosses

nothing   no signs

empty bunk beds / mothers who forget
& cook too much
   GREENS.
just gone / disappeared
cuz they're black & poor   they gone
took a bus / was never heard of again
   OKRA.
somebody heard a child scream & went on
somebody sits up nights dreaming bout
children screaming / their mama's
& somebody else who delights in
watching children struggle to breathe /
fightin
   GREENS.
this animal with visions of dead children
rotting in the woods
children   somewhere disappearing
& the mothers still cry out / dreamin
   OKRA.
mothers always at the windows watching
can't nobody disappear right in fronta yr eyes
nobody
   GREENS.
yet when yr black & poor /
who knows what cd happen to you
we dont seem to be here no way

how cd we disappear if we aint even here
who cd hear us screamin?
    OKRA.
say it's a man with a badge & some candy
say it's a man with a badge & some money
say it's a maniac
cd be more than stars & stripes
gotta be more than sticks & stones
children cant play war /
    GREENS.
when they in one
caint make believe / when they aint
cant imagine they dyin / when they are
cant say what they'll be when they grow up /
cuz they wont
    OKRA.
oh mary dont you weep dont you moan
HOLLAR MAMMA HOLLAR
cuz we black & poor
& children just gone
    GREENS.
disappeared
    OKRA.
we cant find em Jesus we cant even find em
til they seepin in soil
reekin Father gone from this world
    GREENS.
bones bout disappeared
& they lives aint never been
dyin where the earth's awready red in atlanta
    OKRA.
we cant find em Jesus cant find em
dyin cuz they took a bus
& mama cant see that far out her window

the front porch dont go from here to eternity
  GREENS.
& they gone just disappeared
& somebody's walking who shd be crawling
goin round killin who aint never been
cuz they black & poor they disappear
  OKRA.
dont matter how sweet
dont matter how that smile curls up on her face
what he laughed so hard abt to himself the other day
  GREENS.
they gone
  OKRA.
be right back Ma
goin round to the store Daddy
see you later Mother Dear
call you when i get there Nana
& the soil run red
with our dead
  GREENS.
cuz somebody heard their screams & went on ahead
crushing them lil bones / strangling them lil frail
  wails
  OKRA.
 / crying "mama"
& she's looking out the door
sayin to herself / "i wonder where is my child? i
  wonder
where is my child?"
she dont turn the bed back cuz she knows
we're black & poor
& we just disappear   be gone
  GREENS.
oh mary dont you weep dont you moan
HOLLAR HOLLAR HOLLAR

OKRA.
where is my child
where is my child
where is my child
GREENS.
nothing
no signs

(*GREENS leaves dejected and pained on "nothing, no
signs." OKRA takes center stage on her knees, to
begin "we need a god who bleeds." One DANCER
in silhouette behind the backdrop dances
throughout.*)

OKRA.
we need a god who bleeds now
a god whose wounds are not
some small male vengeance
some pitiful concession to humility
a desert swept with dryin marrow in honor of the lord
we need a god who bleeds
spreads her lunar vulva & showers us in shades of
    scarlet
thick & warm like the breath of her
our mothers tearing   to let us   in
this place breaks open
like our mothers bleeding
the planet is heaving   mouring our ignorance
the moon tugs the seas
to hold her/ to hold her
embrace swelling hills/ i am
not wounded i am bleeding to life
we need a god who bleeds now
whose wounds are not the end of anything

(*Strains of "Mood Indigo"* are heard as GREENS approaches to take her knees, to begin "it hasn't always been this way." They speak to one another as the DANCERS appear and disappear as characters or emotional manifestations of the piece. OKRA and GREENS to one another as the dancers appear and disappear as characters or emotional manifestations of the place.*)

GREENS.
it hasnt always been this way
ellington was not a street
robeson no mere memory
du bois walked up my father's stairs
hummed some tune over me
sleeping in the company of men
who changed the world

it wasnt always like this
why ray barretto used to be a side-man
& dizzy's hair was not always grey
i remember   i was there
i listened in the company of men
politics as necessary as collards
music even in our dreams

our house was filled with all kinda folks
our windows were not cement or steel
doors opened like our daddy's arms

---

*Note: Permission to use this music in production must be procured from its copyright owner. Permission to produce FROM OKRA TO GREENS does not include permission to use this music.

held us safe & loved
children growing in the company of men
old southern men & young slick ones
sonny til was not a boy
the clovers no rag-tag orphans
our crooners/ we belonged to a whole world
nkrumah was no foreigner
virgil aikens was not the only fighter

it hasnt always been this way
elington was not a street
   OKRA.
there is something caught in my throat
it is this place
my baby is sleeping
i check to see if she is alive
she does not know about gagging
she does not have this place/ in her throat
she doesnt know where we are
how it sears the membranes
eats the words right outta your mouth
leaves you suckin' pollutants impotence
& failure/
   GREENS.
      a whole race of people cant do nothin'
at the roller disco.
   OKRA.
there is something caught in my throat
it is hard & ugly/ i wd vomit it out
but the malignancy only grows toward
my gut/ & will not come out alive
my child is sleeping
she doesnt know where we are &
some man/ wants to kiss my thighs

roll his tongue around my navel
put his hands all up my ass
& this place is in my throat

       how can i tell him
     there is nothing up my behind/ that
   will get this place
out of my throat.
        (i went to a dangerous place with a man who
        was not there/ cuz he cant do nothin' but
        dial a joke or call for information)
   GREENS.
you cd tell him a few things
       there are dead children out here
       there are desperate women out here
       the sky is falling
  & i am choking to death
cuz of where i am & who we are.
this is the twentieth century.
  (do you think artra skin tone cream will solve
  colored complexion problems during a limited
    nuclear
  engagement/ or
are you stocking up on porcelana?)
   OKRA.
i have this thing in my throat
i ant put no more tongues in my mouth/
no cigarettes/ no tranquilers/ i cant eat   anything
i shoulda kept my damn champagne.
& ask the coke man for something so good/
it would burn this place
outta my soul/ so i cd breathe
& check my daughter who is still sleeping

GREENS.
she thinks unicorns & magnolias
are things to put in her mouth
she dont know where she is yet
she dont know alla black kid's gonna get
is a fist in her mouth or a white man
who says she's arrogant / cuz
she can look him in the eye/ cuz
she dont know where she is.

OKRA.
this thing is in my throat/
exploding just beneath my chin
i told this man my daughter didnt know
where she was/ where i keep my child
there are no white men   with sexual thoughts
about infants/ she'll know better next time
cuz she aint having this place

GREENS.
this gun happy/ watch niggers die-n-fuck
each other to death in style place/ when
they got ads sayin' come & see the Satin Latins /
        but
dress as white gods & goddesses/
she aint here for that.

OKRA.
i am choking to death
                (& some man watched me looking for him
                in the rain & called me later to say
                he saw me in the rain/ looking & couldnt
                do anything about it cuz it was an
                aesthetic thing)
this place is caught in my throat
i would tear it out & let you eat it

but i have a daughter who sleeps well/ & till
somebody comes to help me/ i'll have to keep
swallowing this place/ like the rest of you
    GREENS.
praying you wont have to hold
all yr respect for human beings in yr one closed
    fist
yr one fistfull of fight/ that we'll choke
on this place/ & make it somewhere
we could live.
    OKRA.
        please
        dont send no flowers.
        i dont want no white wine.
        i dont even want a roof over my head.
i want his place out of my throat
    GREENS.
i want james brown to stop singing/ to get the hell
    out the way
& let a man come in.

(*All DANCERS have exited. Only OKRA and
    GREENS are there to comfort one another.*)

    OKRA.
i could sleep with a man
but i'll lay with the souls of black folks
maybe i could grow me something
some azure flower that would smell
like life to me/ a root of some healing spice
might push up from my soils/ if i
dream with the souls of black folks.
    GREENS.
what is invisible is not a man

but the spirits of some who were
bigger is not a black boy yearning for an airplane
but the gaze of our children who dont know
why 'we caint get no satisfaction'.
   OKRA.
i could sleep with a man
i could even sing with a man
but i gotta rise with the souls of black folks
where could the A train take me
i dont know where i'm sposed to go
ellington is not a street.
       & my child knows her world
       is as rich as people in sorrow can spare/
       brash as our bodies in the black forest
but it hasnt always been this way
   GREENS.
i swear/ we were not always missing.

(*With temerity OKRA and GREENS talk about slug's.
   They can see it and point it out in the audience.*)

   GREENS.
i thought i might be in slug's
pharoah waz singin
though he didnt beat his
chest
   OKRA.
carnival rolled outta brooklyn thru the snow
& soho/ right up 7th avenue south
with our wintry american version of the jump-up
   GREENS.
pharoah did know the sun
& tabo screamed over & over
6 tenor players filled the front row
the battles of the horns to commence

OKRA.
but i know this isnt slug's
cuz lee morgan's blood doesnt dot the sawdust
ayler's echoes cant be heard in the john &
sun-ra doesnt work here mondays
GREENS.
i'm not 19 years old either/ in tie-dyed jeans
& pink satin/ watchin 3rd street burn down lil by
    lil
while the yng ones with mouth pieces & brushes
wait to sit in/
OKRA.
this isn't slug's cuz death seems
so far away/ not boomer's where death is sold in
    packages
it's ten years later/
GREENS.
& the changes are transcribed

(*All the FEMALE DANCERS appear abruptly dressed
    in red. They deliver in unison* ("spose I say you're
    leafy and you come in five different tastes") *like
    Vanity 6. GREENS succumbs to their flirtations in
    dance, ignores OKRA, is carried off stage by the
    WOMEN DANCERS.*)

GREENS.
spose i say i know yr leafy
you come in 5 different tastes/ yr edges vary
you have seasons of yr own choosin/ spose
the distance from yr collard to yr mustard
is same as from the width of my field
OKRA.
you know the incidence of greens overdose

is unfortunately internationally unknown
this condition is not due to pesticides war
land-fill overflow or legionnaire's disease
greens overdose might not ever be reported
   GREENS.
/ feels too good/ most victums smile
without knowing why/ but i know   i gotta
o.d. of greens/ i'm sufferin so
my pods are gleamin/ ready to jump out
the vertical/ into the greens diagonal
   OKRA.
oh
   GREENS.
greens is planting which ever angle suits you
when i am wearin my grey tie & the doc shoes/
come this way

(*OKRA wanders stage dejected. Delivers the following
   front stage left in spotlight, as if GREENS were in
   audience.*)

   OKRA.
when you disappeared
the night sat in my mouth
like a rush of a holler
how i dug my feet into the sidewalk
when mama tried to take me to the new school
how i refused to under stand freedom rides
& cheap lunch counters too good for me
with raw yolk across my forehead &
catsup streamin from my temples
a parody of my blood
creepin thru the furrows of my lips
tastin so much like yr tongue

when you disappeared
a tremendous silence shook
my body til my bones split ·
i hadta   grab my sinews from the mouths of bats
none of the nice boys wd dance with me
my hair turned back
i looked like the child found in
the chicken coop after 13 years
i knew no language
my fingers had never held bread
i cd not walk
when you disappeared
the moon cracked in a ugly rupture
fell a cursin for the night to catch her

(*GREENS re-enters, aware that he has hurt OKRA deeply. In an adagio duet, they make up. On the line "so we do it all of it", raggae music comes up.*)

GREENS.
wd you like to make love tonite
landscapes can be tawdry
but the horizon at tamaris hasn't known a cheap
    moment
come with me to the kasbah   or the tin palace
but wd you like to make love tonite
something happened on lenox/ the train came
you know what i mean/ it waznt the A train though
ellington waz looking good in brooklyn & it waznt
the coney island express with the horses ferris
    wheels
& junkies on the failin boardwalks/ but the train
    did come
& it waz good cuz i waz cold

wd you like to make love tonite
there's a place we love & tony davis doesnt work
    there
    OKRA.
give me a lullabye
    GREENS.
you cd hear it
between blue brown   walls i call my own
where butterflies & great ladies take respite/ you
cd rest on flowers of silk/ where i wanna make love
with you
so all the trains & vamps/ my runs & songs
the steeplechase   hawker/ intervals of major &
    doubly
augmented sighs/ the cafe in knesset where the sun
    makes the
meat hotter than an oven/ even the angolan exiles
    in lisbon
cd drink with us again
    GREENS.
if you were to hold me tonite
everywhere we've been wd lay on me so
i might only kiss you/ like the night all we did
    waz kiss
all nite long/ but see/ i really wanna make love
    tonite
how we live our lives/ so we do all of it

(*All DANCERS re-enter. There is a festive reggae dance
    throughout the following.*)

    OKRA.
i've been married to bob marley
for at least 17 years

i usedta call him smokey robinson
it's hard to remember i
waz underage at the time of our union &
changed my birthdate
so much i cant count the years
only the satisfaction

bob marley is my husband
whether our marriage is legal has to do
with where you live & if you think highly
of haile selassie/ the lion of judah
my children are hiding in toco forest
they swing on their rasta red hair / climbin
jungle jims of lapis under the supervision
of the good colored men from uranus/
where all colored men are kindergarten teachers/
where they sing my husband's songs
where we exodus-ed to outta here
where natural mystics
be jammin alla the time
they be raining joy on everybody house
i tell you no lie

bob marley take care of me
cuz he wanna give me some love
been knockin on my door threee year
& he still here for sure
he jump
he scream
he shake he head
he close he eye
he be in the promised land
he wait for me on star
he blaze

he sing
he wanna jam it wit me
he dont wait in vain
he in the movement of the people
he jump
he scream
he shake he head
he close he eye
he head twirl from london to canal street
he braids fall from the sun
he see me
he lay his mark here
i reach for the world
he give it to me
i work   i rest   i love him in the air
i cd fondle the sky
watch kingston eclipse guiltiness

 in the name of the lord
the lion of judah
david's warriors
rise up rise up fallen fighters
show me the promised land
show me round the universe
our fathers' lands
rise up
announce the coming of the kingdom's rightful heirs
i climbin to the moon on the rasta thruway
our fathers' lands
risin up
    GREENS.
the land even sing & jump
the sky want to jam all thru the day
the stars forget they weakness
& dance

OKRA & GREENS. (*dancing*)
rise up fallen fighters
unfetter the stars
dance with the universe

(*Violently interupting the festivities, a volley of
machine gun shots rings out. The music stops. The
DANCERS become guerrilla fighters. Everyone is
thrown a weapon from off stage. A battle scene is
enacted. The players quietly assemble in defensive
positions back stage. GREENS sits, as if on watch,
and delivers 'i must go to La Costa." OKRA trium-
phantly approaches him and begins her lines. They
are partners in struggle. She motions for everyone
to leave as if she has a secret. GREENS and OKRA
throw their weapons to departing dancers. OKRA
informs GREENS of her pregnancy. He doesn't
believe it at first. She must convince him. They ac-
cept new idea. Angolan (African) music comes up.
DANCERS enter on "present yourself."*)

OKRA.
our language   is tactile
colored & wet
our tongues speak
these words
we dance
these words
sing em like we mean it/
      do it to em stuff drag punch & cruise it
to em/ live it/ the poem/
our visions are our own
our truth no less violent than necessary
to make

our daughters' dreams
as real as mensis
   GREENS.
the earth hums some song of her own . . .
   GREENS.
i tried to tell the doctor
i really tried to tell her
tween the urine test & the internal exam/
when her fingers were circling my swollen cervix
i tried
to tell her the baby was confused
the baby doesnt know
she's not another poem.
you see/ i was working on a major piece of fiction
at the time of conception
"doctor/ are you listening?"
had just sent 4 poems off to the *new yorker*
& was copy-editing a collection of plays
during those "formative first twelve weeks"
there were opening parties
all of which involved me & altered the poor baby's
aminiotic bliss/
     "doctor/ the baby doesnt think she shd
     come out that way!"
i mean/ she thinks she shd come up/ not down
into the ground/ she thinks her mother makes up
   things
nice things ugly things but made up things
   nonetheless
unprovable irrational subjective fantastic things
not subject to objective or clinical investigation/
she believes the uterine cave is a metaphor
     "doctor/ you have to help me"
this baby wants to jump out of my mouth

at a reading someplace/
the baby's refusing to come out/ down
she wants to come out a spoken word
but i have no way to reach her
how can i convince her
to drop her head & take on the world like the rest
   of us
she cant move up til she comes out
      "whatever shall i do? i've been pregnant
      a long time"
i finally figured out what to say
to this literary die-hard of a child of mine
"you are an imperative my dear"/ & i felt her startle
toward my right ovary then i said/ "as an imperative
it is incumbent upon you to present yrself"

(*During the following, ENTIRE CAST does lively
   modern dance with Latin and African references as
   OKRA and GREENS acknowledge their global off-
   spring. The ENTIRE CAST dances off, OKRA car-
   ried away in GREEN's arms. Music stays up until
   they are out of sight. OKRA and GREENS re-enter
   from opposite sides of stage.*)

   OKRA.
i have a daughter/ mozambique
   GREENS.
i have a son/ angola
   OKRA.
our twins
   GREENS.
salvador & johannesbourg/ cannot speak
the same language

but we fight the same old men/ in the new world
   OKRA.
we are so hungry for the morning
we're trying to feed our children the sun
   GREENS.
but a long time ago/ we boarded ships/ locked in
depths of seas our spirits/ kisst the earth
on the atlantic side of nicaragua costa rica
our lips traced the edges of cuba puerto rico
   OKRA.
charleston & savannah/ in haiti
we embraced &
   GREENS.
made children of the new world
but old men spit on us/ shackled our limbs
   OKRA.
but for a minute
   GREENS.
out cries are   the panama canal/ the yucatan
we poured thru more sea/ more ships/ to manila
ah ha we're back again
   OKRA.
everybody in manila awready speaks spanish
   GREENS.
the old men sent for the archbishop of canterbury
   OKRA.
"can whole continents be excommunicated?"
   GREENS.
"what wd happen to the children?"
   OKRA.
"wd their allegiance slip over the edge?"
   GREENS.
"dont worry bout lumumba/ don't even think bout

ho chi minh/ the dead cant procreate"
so say the old men
   OKRA.
but i have a daughter/ la havana
   GREENS.
i have a son/ nairobi
   OKRA.
our twins
   GREENS.
santiago & brixton/ cannot speak
the same language
yet we fight the same old men
   OKRA.
the ones who think helicopters rhyme with hunger
   GREENS.
who think patrol boats can confiscate a people
   OKRA.
the ones whose dreams are full of none of our
children
   GREENS.
they see mae west & harlow in whittled white cafes
near managua/ listening to primitive rhythms in
jungles near pétionville
   OKRA.
with bejewled benign natives
ice skating in abidjian
   GREENS.
unaware of the rest of us in chicago
   OKRA.
all the dark urchins
rounding out the globe/ primitively whispering
the earth is not flat old men
   GREENS.
there is no edge

OKRA.
no end to the new world
   GREENS.
cuz i have a daughter/ trinidad
   OKRA.
i have a son/ san juan
   GREENS.
our twins
   OKRA.
capetown & palestine/ cannot speak the same
language/ but we fight the same old men
   GREENS.
the same men who thought the earth waz flat
   OKRA.
go on over the edge/ go on over the edge old men
   GREENS.
you'll see us in luanda. or the rest of us
in chicago
   OKRA.
it be hot   & then again not
breeze know how to cool
the burnin
   GREENS.
when the sun force us to twitch
punctuate the air
wit alla this/
   OKRA.
the breeze she
fan our behind/ tickle the bosoms   let the music
free out out soul rush
up from the waves/
   GREENS.
no matter
no matter the seaweed   tease

thru legs   make us want/
   OKRA.
make us want
to swing with the horizon
   GREENS.
so easy   so easy   to swim to swing
   OKRA.
to stroke hard to breathe deep
   GREENS.
but the sun she want us   to twitch
   OKRA.
she love to watch us sway alla sudden
   GREENS.
throw the leg round there/ hips put so to the sun
winds like opium lovers/
   OKRA.
the winds get in our blood
run us to the sea/ the sea she want it all
   GREENS.
the sun she want us hot
but it be hot & then again not
   OKRA.
the sea she want it all
   GREENS.
& she keep comin back/ she lick our toes
cuz the sun she want us so/ but it be hot
& then again
not

(*All exit. Music stays up for curtain call.*)

The End

COSTUMES

African costumes for dancers
Brazilian costumes for dancers
Contemporary American costumes for dancers
Guerilla-looking tattered costumes
Carnival fantastic costumes for dancers
OKRA and GREENS stay in same clothes throughout.
  GREENS in white linen pants and white Caribbean
  dress shirt. OKRA in wide orange raw silk skirt
  with plaid raw silk top.
No shoes except for urban scenes; then, only for
  dancers.

PROPS

Uzi machine guns

Suggested Music for FROM OKRA TO GREENS

Pre-show
"Usted Abuso" — Celie Cruz & Willie Colon
"Private Dancer" — Tina Turner
"F Troop Rides Again" — Lester Bowie
"I Wanta Love You & Treat You Right" — Bob Marley

Opening dance: traditional Yoruban drums or Brazilian percussion samsa.
Saxophone solo: "Nonaah" — Roscoe Mitchell
Okra's speech beginning on p. 12 — "Ribbons in the Sky" — Stevie Wonder
Greens p. 14 — any piece by Leci Brondão
Dancers p. 18 — "I Would Die For You" — Prince
Dancers p. 25 — "Indent" — Cecil Taylor
Greens pp. 25–26 — "La Vie en Rose" — Edith Piaf
Dancers p. 27 — Ravi Shankar sitar music
Dancers p. 28 — extended version, "F Troop Rides Again"
Okra p. 28 — "Coq Qualité" — Les Maxels
Dancers p. 33 — extended version, "Nonaah"
Okra p. 37 — "This is the Universe" — Jeanne Lee & Gunter Hompel
Greens p. 38 — "Mood Indigo" — Duke Ellington
Okra pp. 39–42 — "In & Out" — Sonny Sharrock
Okra p. 42 — "Take the A Train" — Duke Ellington
Greens p. 43 — "African Ballad — Anthony Davis
Greens & female dancers — "What's Love Got to Do With It?" — Tina Turner
Greens & Okra adagio p. 46 — "She's Hot" — Smokey Robinson
Dancers — "Exodus a Bad Girl" — Bob Marley
Dancers p. 50 — Angolan Freedom songs
Entire cast p. 52 — "Controversy" — Prince
p. 54 — "Proud Mary" — Tina Turner
p. 55 — "Libertad" — Eddie Palmieri

Also By
Ntozake Shange

Theatre

For Colored Girls Who Have Considered Suicide/
When the Rainbow is Enuf

Spell #7

A Photograph: Lovers in Motion

Boogie Woogie Landscapes

Poetry

nappy edges

some men (with Wopo Holup)

A Daughter's Geography

Matrilineal poems

Fiction

Sassafras, Cypress & Indigo

Melissa & Smith

Betsey Brown

Please visit our website **samuelfrench.com** for complete
descriptions and licensing information